Paper, Scissors, Sculpt!

Creating Cut-and-Fold Animals

Paper, Scissors, Sculpt!

Creating Cut-and-Fold Animals

BEN A. GONZALES

Creator of the Gupit-Gupit[SM] technique

Sterling Publishing Co., Inc.
New York

With thanks to:
Gayong Dagat Gonzales
Neil Garcia

Library of Congress Cataloging-in-Publication Data
Gonzales, Ben A.
  Paper, scissors, sculpt! : creating cut-and-fold animals / Ben A. Gonzales.
    p. cm.
  Includes index.
  ISBN 1-4027-1821-7
  1. Paper work. 2. Paper sculpture. 3. Animals in art. I. Title.

TT870.G57 2005
745.54—dc22

2004025982

Paper Sculptor: Ben A. Gonzales
Illustrations: Matang B. Gonzales
Book Design: Dawn DeVries Sokol
Editor: Rodman Pilgrim Neumann

10 9 8 7 6 5 4 3 2 1
Published by Sterling Publishing Co., Inc.
387 Park Avenue South, New York, NY 10016
© 2005 by Ben A. Gonzales and Matang B. Gonzales
Distributed in Canada by Sterling Publishing
C/o Canadian Manda Group, 165 Dufferin Street
Toronto, Ontario, Canada M6K 3H6
Distributed in Great Britain and Europe by Chris Lloyd at Orca Book
Services, Stanley House, Fleets Lane, Poole BH15 3AJ, England
Distributed in Australia by Capricorn Link (Australia) Pty. Ltd.
P.O. Box 704, Windsor, NSW 2756, Australia

Sterling ISBN 1-4027-1821-7

For information about custom editions, special sales, premium and
corporate purchases, please contact Sterling Special Sales
Department at 800-805-5489 or specialsales@sterlingpub.com.

Contents

Projects

Introduction

"YOU ARE A MASTER!"
—Cheng Hou-Tien, Chinese Master Paper-Cutter, Freehold, NJ

Ancient China, circa A.D. 105: Tsai Lung, Caretaker of the Imperial Library, did not like the confusing clutter of leaves, clay, silk, wood, stones, bamboo, and bark that lay on the library shelves. Experimenting with a variety of materials, he invented the very first example of modern paper from the bark of the mulberry tree. Soon after that, fans, toys, decorations, and Chinese kites began to appear.

From sixth century to fourteenth century Japan, the elegant art of paper folding evolved with the development of a sturdier paper. They called it origami; it involved folding a sheet of paper into geometric animal or abstract forms for recreation or packaging.

Fast forward to the twentieth century: in a remote Philippine village near the shadow of an active volcano, a child marveled at the decorative shapes that his babysitter had folded from palm fronds. Although intricate in design, they were simple to make. The image left a permanent impression. *I was that child.*

That early experience was a catalyst for the concept of *Paper, Scissors, Sculpt! Creating Cut-and-Fold Animals.* I created the Gupit-Gupit[SM] technique of one-piece paper sculpture. I use scissors and mat knife to create three-dimensional animal forms that seem complex but are really quite simple. As an art educator, I developed teaching techniques that allow children and adults to become aware of the sense of touch. The ability to think in three dimensions is invaluable in numerous professions, such as carpentry, engineering, architecture, sewing, fashion design, surgery, dentistry.

Sculpting with cut-and-folded paper has impacted my life and the lives of many. I hope this book will inspire you to take the first step on a journey into the third dimension.

—Master Ben A. Gonzales

FOR PARENTS AND TEACHERS

"It is extremely exciting because there is an element of chance and surprise which adults and children enjoy. It also involves many skills important in the art field, such as measuring, folding, planning, and color." —Doris Petrochoko, Art Teacher, Oxford, CT

Intellectual concepts and aesthetic ideas can be easily absorbed when presented visually. The economy and tactile qualities of paper make it an ideal medium for channeling creative energies in the home or in the classroom.

Each project in this book is designed to build skills that prepare for the next sculpture project. The follow-up patterns help reinforce newly acquired abilities. Jumping from one-star to three-star projects defeats this purpose.

Be aware that children have different levels of hand and eye coordination. Allowance should be made for new creative interpretations.

These projects can be used to supplement typical subjects taught in the classroom, such as geography, biology, and the environment. They provide a creative, stress-free respite that can enhance the day's lessons.

Creating Cut-and-Fold Sculptures with Paper and Scissors:

Gupit-Gupit^{SM}

Gupit-Gupit (goo'peet-goo'peet) *n* 1: The art of paper sculpture made from one piece of paper. Gupit-Gupit means "cut-cut" in Tagalog, the national language of the Philippines. 2: Gupit-Gupit is not origami, which is geometrically folded paper. Gupit-Gupit utilizes scoring and cutting as well as folding. 3 Gupit-Gupit is an original creation by Master Ben A. Gonzales, a native from Polangui, Albay, on the island of Luzon, in the Philippines.

Symbols

_____ **Cut** with scissors or mat knife.

- - - - - - - - - - - - **Front Score.** The score line is on the front of the paper: Bend the paper away from the score line so the paper bends backward.

· · · · · · · · · · · · **Back Score:** Bend the paper up from the score line; the score line is then at the back or bottom of the V and the paper bends forward.

- · - · - · - · - · - · **Soft Score:** Paper can be bent either way. This is useful for a flexible bend on the score line that won't tear.

//////////// **Glue** Area.

 **Bend** in the direction of the arrow.

Achievement Ratings

★ Basic for beginners. All ages.

★ ★ Familiar with basics.

★ ★ ★ Familiar with basics plus experience.

★ ★ ★ ★ Inspired.

Supply List

BASIC SUPPLIES

Minimal supply list for the budget conscious:

PAPER & PENCILS

80 lb. slightly stiff drawing paper. Try acid-free paper for durability. Use any pencil that does not smear too much.

SCISSORS

All-metal blades. Must open all the way to be effective for scoring.

PUSH PINS

For transferring score lines.

ADHESIVE

White glue or glue sticks.

MAT KNIFE

For adults, and children with close supervision only.

OPTIONAL SUPPLIES

TRACING WHEEL

For transferring score lines and adding textures.

THINNING SHEARS

For adding textures like feathers or hair.

TAPE

Permanent tape to repair mistakes and removable tape to hold parts in place while gluing.

COLOR

Experiment with media.

Basic Techniques

How to Copy Patterns

METHOD 1: Use a photocopy machine.
METHOD 2: Tape the pattern to a bright window and trace.
METHOD 3: Trace using a light box (a box with a glass top and a bulb underneath).

How to Transfer Back Scores

METHOD 1: Trace the back score lines using a bright window, as above.

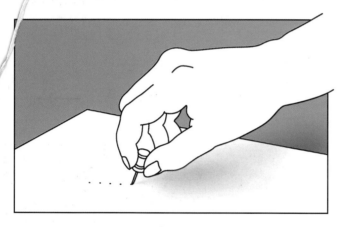

METHOD 2: Trace the score lines by making pinholes.

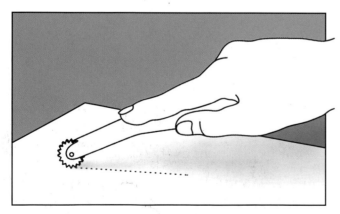

METHOD 3: Use a tracing wheel.

How to Apply White Glue

1 A very small amount of glue is needed to join two pieces of paper. Excess glue wets and wrinkles the paper and delays adhesion. To avoid releasing too much glue, do *not* squeeze the glue bottle and apply directly to the pattern.

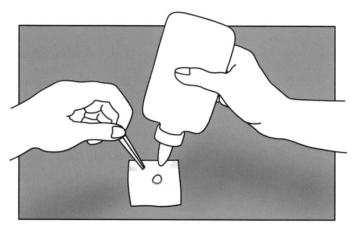

2 Instead, place a drop of glue on a scrap of paper, and then pick up a bit of glue with a folded piece of paper shaped like a toothpick.

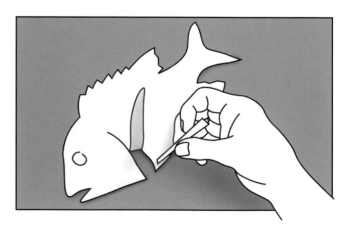

3 Apply the glue quickly, evenly, and sparing. Press the pieces together immediately. It should hold within seconds. Practice!

How to Hold the Scissors and Mat Knife

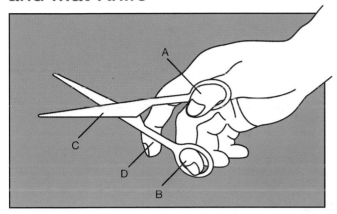

Cutting

The position of thumb (A) and second finger (B) opens the blade wider so the cut can be made in the (C) area. Index finger (D) steadies the blade as it moves up and down. Avoid scissors that do not open all the way

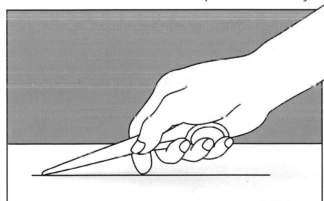

Soft Scoring

1 In soft scoring, cover the work area with a semi-soft padding like a magazine, notepad, or sketch pad.

2 Close the scissors and hold them firmly but gently.

3 Let your hand remain relaxed until pressure is needed to soft score.

4 A soft score line can be bent or folded both ways without tearing.

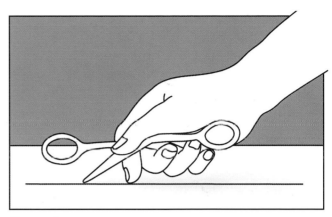

Scoring

1 Open the scissors all the way and hold them gently. Let your hand remain relaxed until pressure is needed to score.

2 Scissors are always pulled (not pushed) over the score line.

3 Paper is always bent or folded *opposite to the score line*.

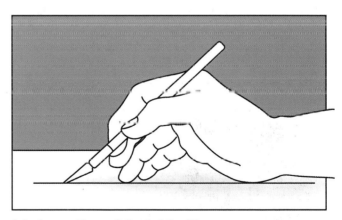

Using the Mat Knife

Optional for adults and older children with supervision only. Knife is pulled (never pushed) over the score line. Let your grip on the knife be relaxed until pressure is needed to cut the score. Always keep the other hand away from the path of the knife hand.

Basic Techniques

How to Score and Bend the Paper

1 Cover the work area with a piece of cardboard.

2 Copy the pattern. Transfer the back scores.

3 Cut out the pattern.

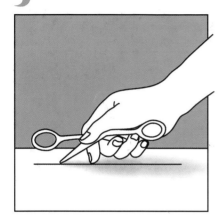

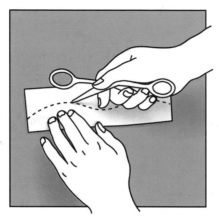

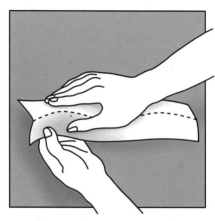

4 Hold the scissors open for scoring. Scissors that do not open all the way cannot be used for scoring.

5 Pull (never push) the scissors blade carefully over the score line. Apply just enough pressure to mark the score line. *Practice!*

6 Bend the paper *opposite* to the score (score will be on outside) with short, gentle strokes, moving both hands together from left to . . .

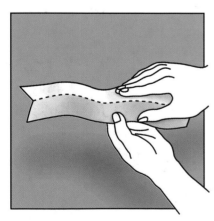

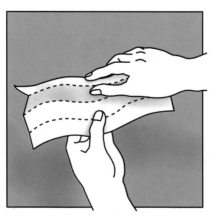

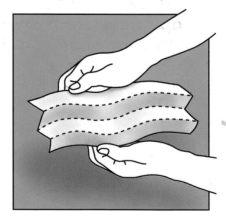

7 . . . right. Repeat as needed. If the paper does not bend easily, the score may be too light. Practice.

8 MULTIPLE SCORES: Proceed in the same way, but *flatten* the paper between each bend.

9 Rebend all the scores at the same time. *Practice!*

How to Soft Score

The soft score makes it possible to fold the paper one way and then the opposite way without tearing it.

1 Cover the work area with a semi-soft padding like a magazine or a sketch pad.

2 Copy the practice pattern below or make your own.

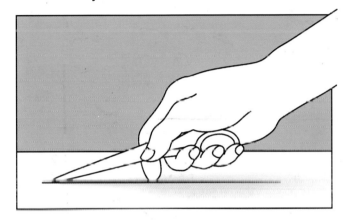

3 Hold the scissors closed for soft scoring. Press down gently and pull the scissors over the score line so as to make a groove. The aim is to compress the paper fibers. See the whale on pages 32–35.

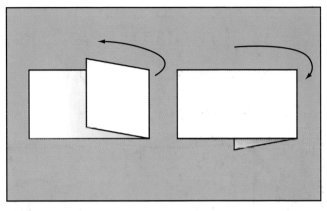

Folding

4 Fold the paper one way. Crease, then fold the opposite way. Crease again. If it does not fold easily *on the score line*, go over it again. *Practice!*

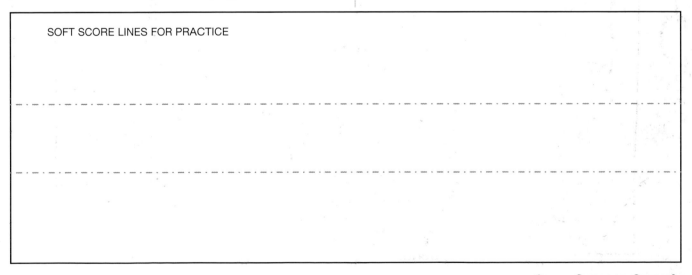

SOFT SCORE LINES FOR PRACTICE

Curve Scores

supplies
80 lb paper
scissors

symbols

cut ——

front
score ----

back
score ....

FRONT SCORE

FRONT SCORE

MULTIPLE SCORES (FRONT AND BACK)

How to Use This Book

Never be afraid of making mistakes.

Don't skip over projects.

Take your time. Patience and practice will bring success.

Experiment with color. Follow your intuition.

Snake A

Snake A ★

1 Copy the pattern the same size as on the pattern page.

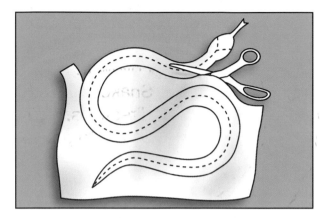

2 Cut along the outline of the pattern.

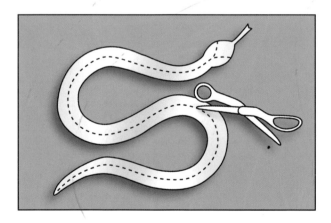

3 Score carefully along the score line with scissors. Remember to pull scissors, not push, when scoring.

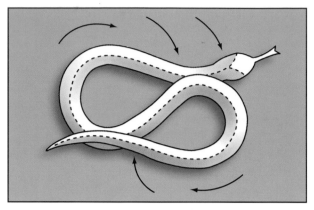

4 Bend the score line so the paper moves. (See arrows.) Do it carefully and gradually.

5 Continue bending along the score. Repeat a few times. Caution: Let the paper move by itself without forcing it.

6 Final phase. Curl the tongue. See arrow.

Snake B

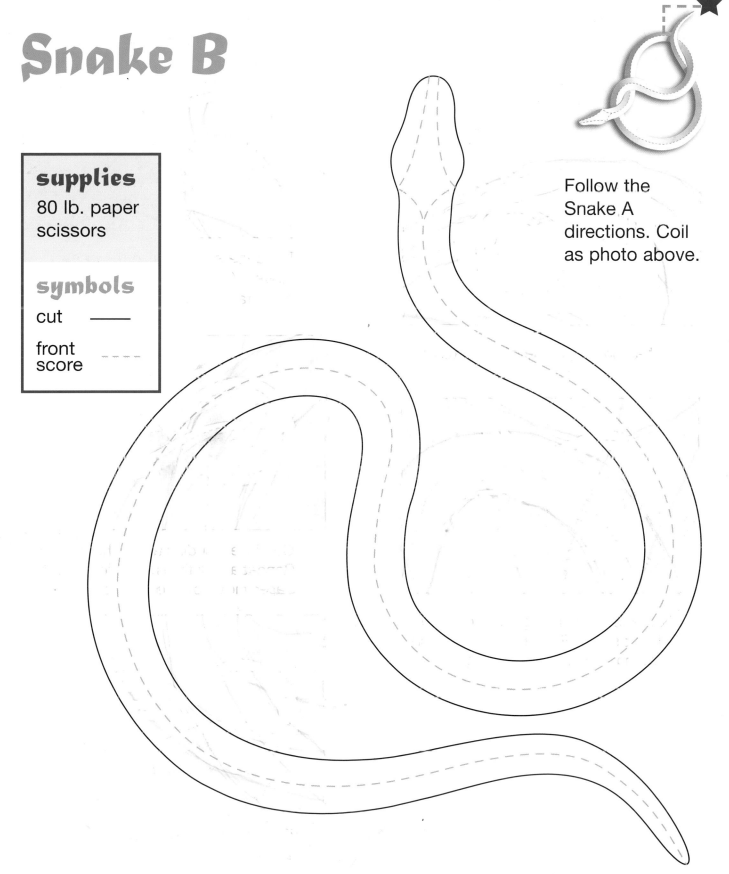

supplies

80 lb. paper
scissors

symbols

cut ———

front
score - - - -

Follow the
Snake A
directions. Coil
as photo above.

Snake C

supplies

80 lb. paper
scissors

symbols

cut ————

front
score - - - - -

Follow
the Snake A
directions, then
coil as photo at
top of page.

Salamander

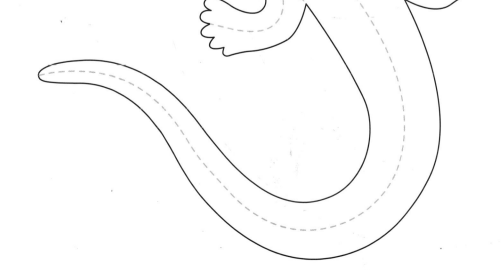

The Salamander is a follow-up to the Snake. Use the basic Snake A directions to create other animals.

Bend the legs down so that it will stand.

Bat

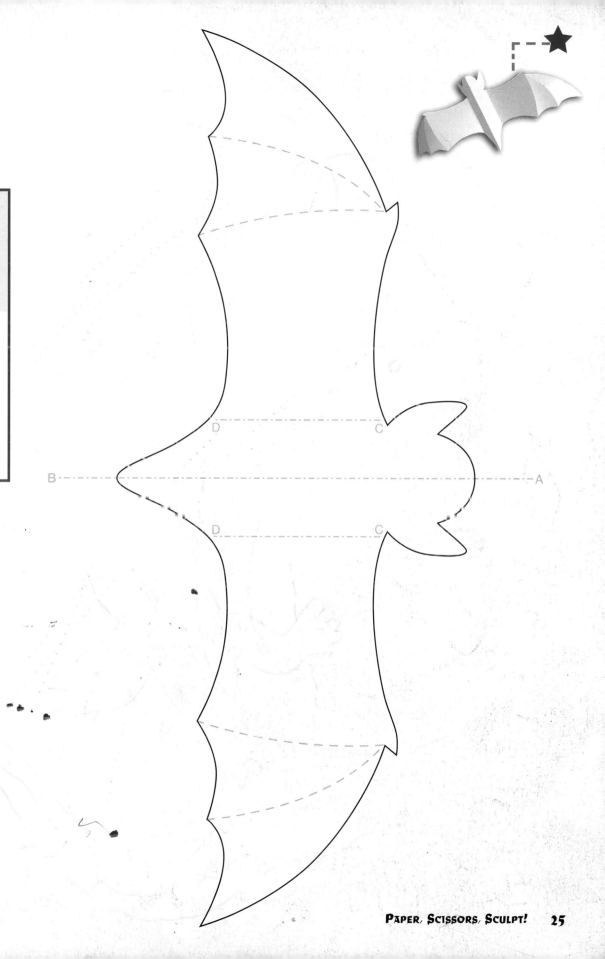

supplies
80 lb. paper
scissors
color

symbols

cut ———

front
score - - - - -

soft
score —·—·—·—

B · — · — · — · — · — · — · — · — · — · — · — · — · — A

D   C

D   C

Bat ★

1 Copy the pattern at the same size.

2 Cut along the outline of the pattern.

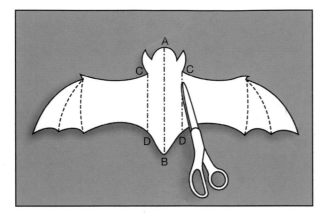

3 Soft score AB and CD. Use a padded surface like a magazine or notebook.

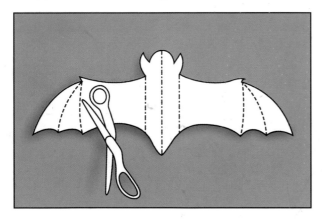

4 Front score the rest of the score lines.

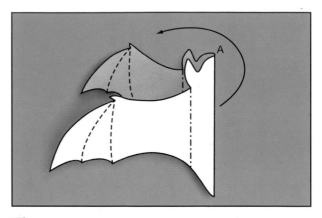

5 Fold the soft score AB one way only.

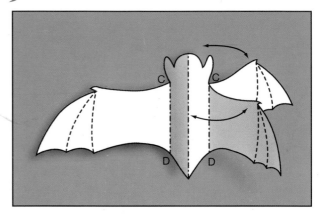

6 Fold the soft scores CD both ways a few times. This will make the wings flap back and forth.

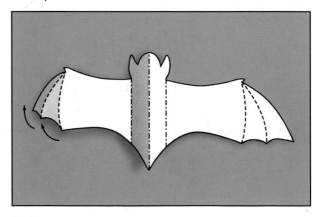

7 Bend the rest of the front scores. Color as you desire.

8 FLY THE BAT. Then try the Butterfly on the next page.

Butterfly

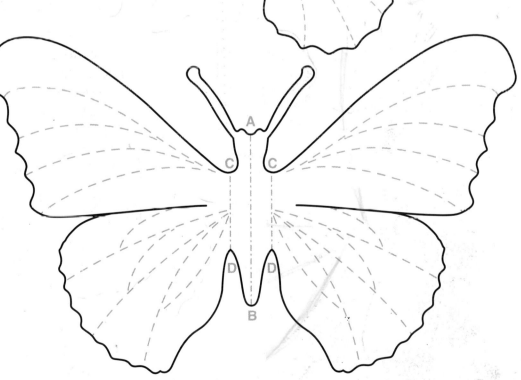

steps

1 Use the
directions
for the Bat.

2 Use brilliant
iridescent
colors.

Shark

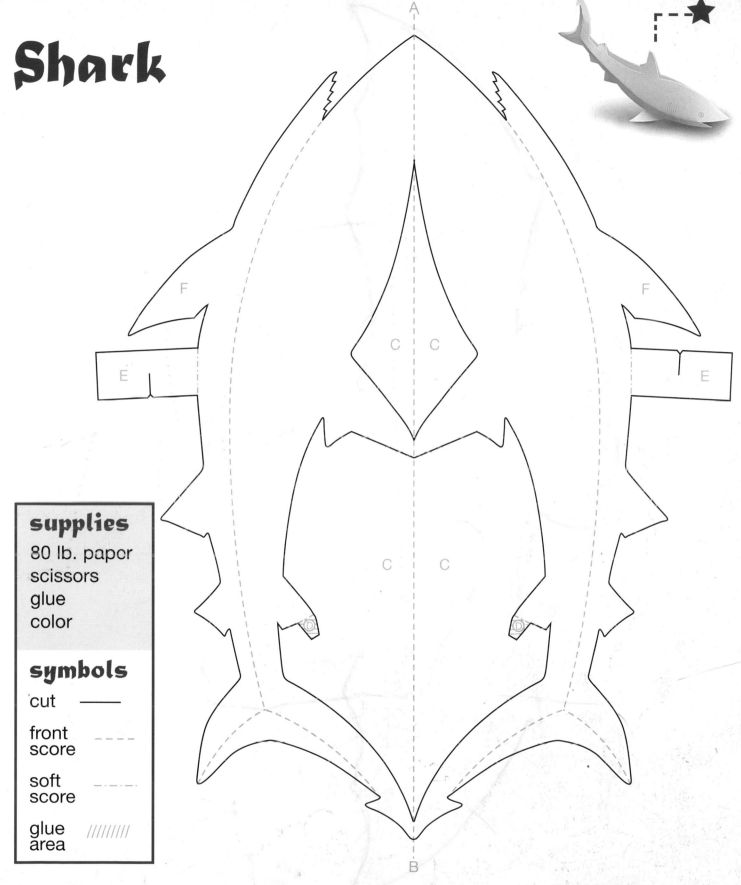

A

F   F

E   E

C   C

C   C

D   D

B

supplies

80 lb. paper
scissors
glue
color

symbols

cut ——————

front
score   - - - - - -

soft
score   —·—·—·—

glue   ////////
area

Shark ★

1 Copy the pattern at the same size.

2 Score AB carefully. Use a ruler to guide the scissors.

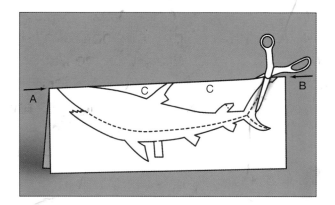

3 Fold AB. Cut out parts labeled C.

4 Open the pattern flat. Cut the outline.

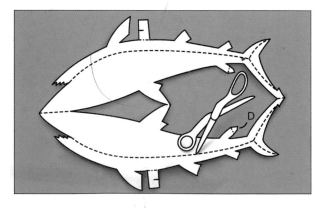

5 Score. Note the soft score on tab D.

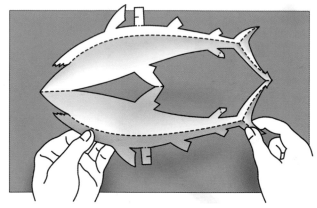

6 Bend the scores gently and carefully.

7 Optional: Add color before gluing tab D.

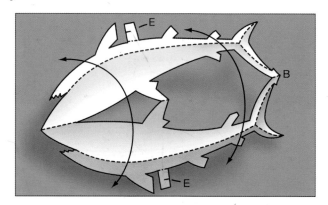

8 Fold AB. Let the belly tabs, E, overlap.

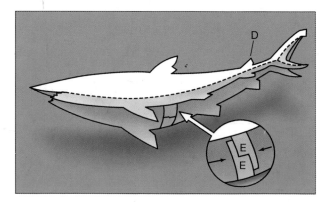

9 Put a small amount of glue on the dorsal fin D. Join the two slits on the E tabs.

10 Bend out the pectoral fins, F. Follow up with the Swordfish.

Swordfish

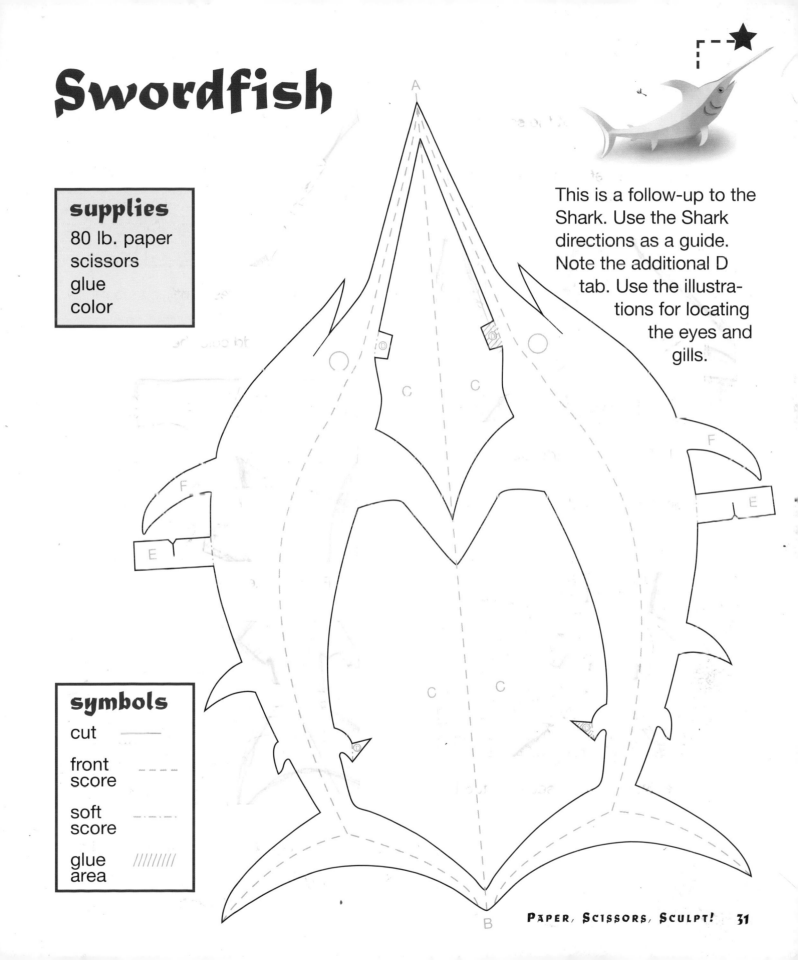

supplies

80 lb. paper
scissors
glue
color

This is a follow-up to the Shark. Use the Shark directions as a guide. Note the additional D tab. Use the illustrations for locating the eyes and gills.

symbols

cut ————

front
score ------

soft
score —·—·—

glue
area //////////

A

C C

F

E

F

E

C C

B

Whale

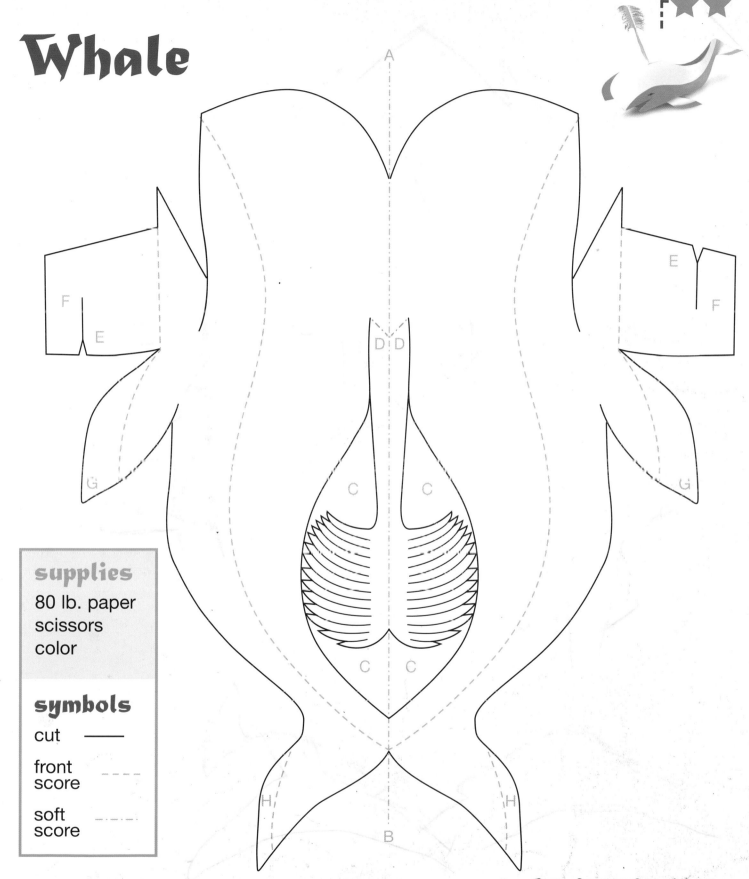

supplies

80 lb. paper
scissors
color

symbols

cut ——————

front
score - - - - - - -

soft
score -·-·-·-·-·-

Whale ★★

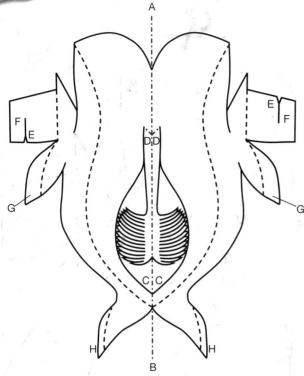

1 Copy the pattern at the same size.

2 Cut the pattern outline. Do not cut into area C yet.

3 Soft score AB. Soft score D.

4 Score body and fins as marked.

5 Fold AB. Crease sharply.

6 Open the pattern and fold AB again, but the opposite way. Crease.

7 Fold AB again so that the pattern lines are on the outside.
NOTE: Steps 5, 6, and 7 are very important.

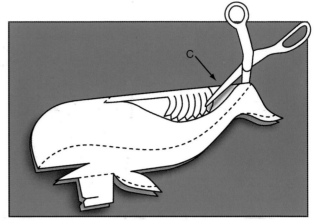

8 Keep the pattern folded. Carefully cut out area C.

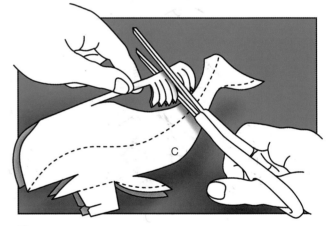

9 Cut into the water spray. Do not cut too far, and do not bend the spout stem.

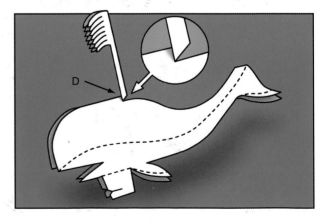

10 Fold D. Crease sharply.

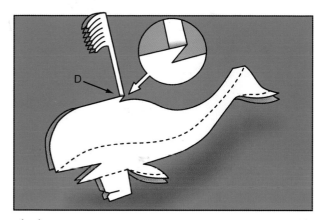

11 Fold D again, but the opposite way. Crease sharply.

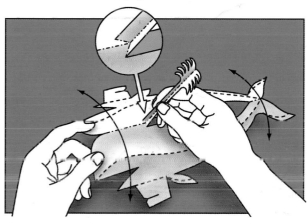

12 TOP VIEW—Raising the spout: Reverse fold the spout stem while slowly raising it up so it bends at D. At the same time, fold the body.

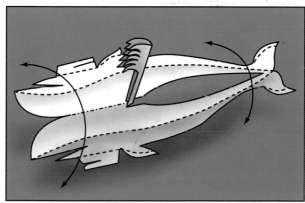

13 TOP VIEW—Continue these two movements until the spout stem is upright.

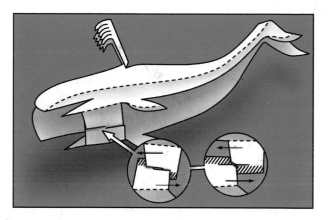

14 UNDERSIDE VIEW—Insert the tie tab slits together (F). The shaded part of the tie-tabs should be on the inside when it is fully engaged.

15 Bend the fins out. Keep the spout stem folded slightly, but keep the water-spout open.

Fish A

 Fish A ★★

1 Copy the pattern at the same size.

2 Transfer the back scores.

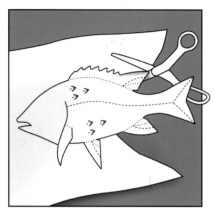

3 Cut out the pattern.

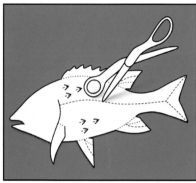

4 Score.

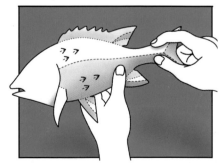

5 Bend all the scores.

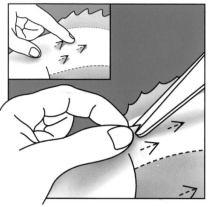

6 To cut a scale: Pinch the score on the scale. Cut with the scissors. Bend up the scales (see inset).

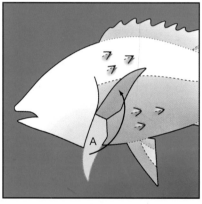

7 Fold up the pectoral fin A, so that it touches the body of the fish. Optional: Apply color now. Let dry. Color the back of fin A. Let dry.

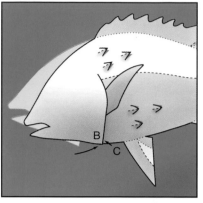

8 Bend the head down over the base of the pectoral fin until B covers C. Put glue under B. Stick it to C.

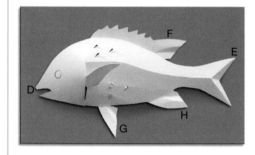

9 To mount to a cardboard background:
a. Mark the position of the tip of the fish nose D and tail end E on the background.
b. Apply glue under the nose D and let it dry.
c. Repeat with the tail tip E. Let it dry.
d. Bend the other fins away from the background so that they stand out, (F, G, and H).
e. Carefully draw in the eye.

Fish B

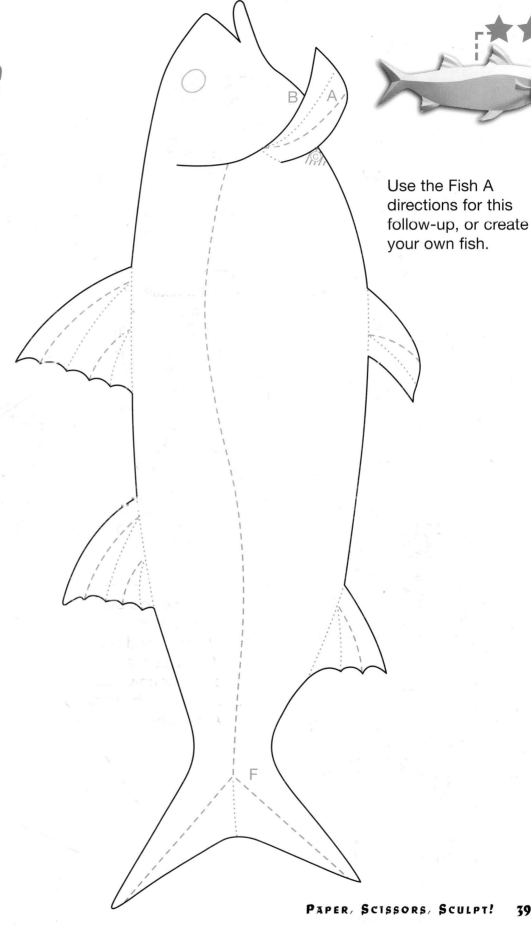

supplies

80 lb. paper
scissors
glue
color

symbols

cut ———

front
score - - - -

back
score ·········

glue
area //////////

Use the Fish A
directions for this
follow-up, or create
your own fish.

B   A

©

F

Bear

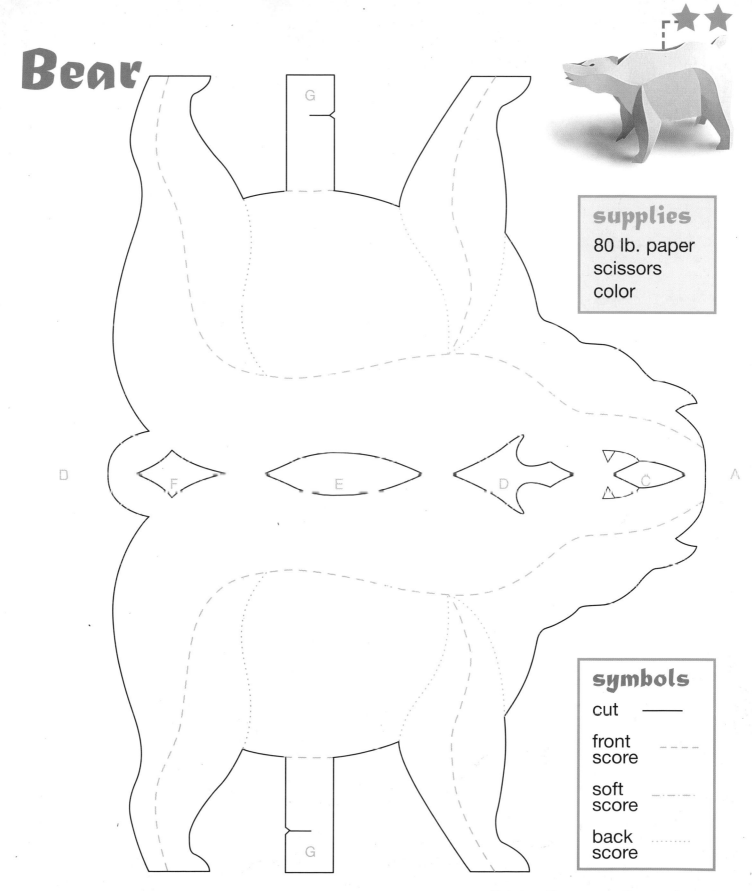

supplies

80 lb. paper
scissors
color

G

D   F   E   D   C   A

symbols

cut ——————

front
score - - - - - -

soft
score -·-·-·-·-

back
score ··········

G

Bear ★ ★

1 Copy the pattern.

2 Transfer the back scores.

3 Score AB.

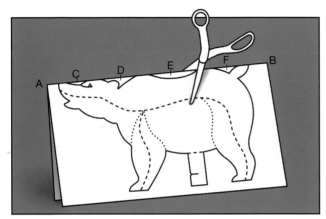

4 Fold AB and crease it carefully.

5 Keep the paper folded. Cut out parts C, D, E, and F.

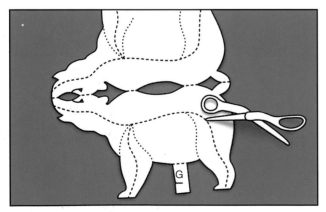

6 Open the pattern flat. Cut out the Bear.

7 Score. Soft score the joint of tab G.

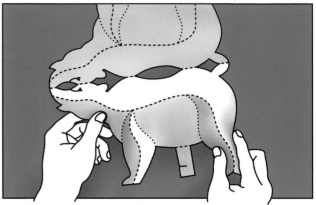

8 Bend the scores carefully.

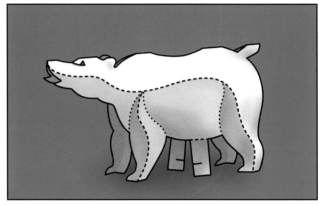

9 Now fold the two sides of the body together.

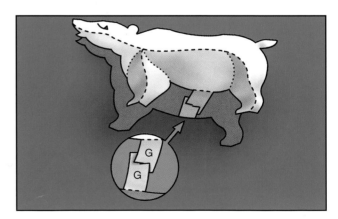

10 Option: Color as desired.

11 Attach the G tabs. Bend out the ears.

Hippopotamus

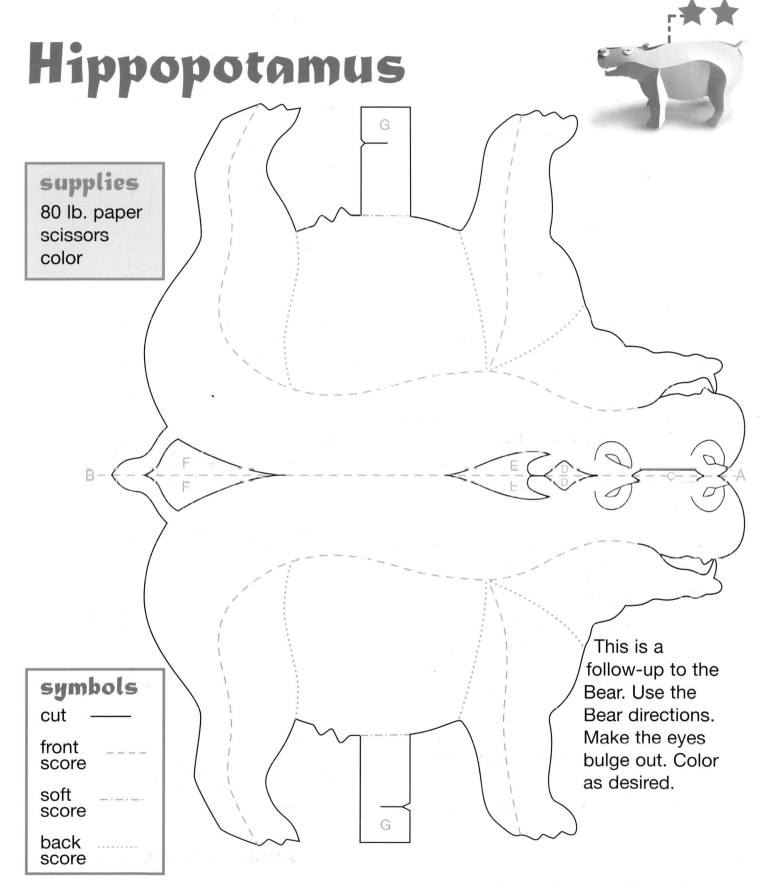

G

B   F   E   D   C   A
     F   E   D

This is a
follow-up to the
Bear. Use the
Bear directions.
Make the eyes
bulge out. Color
as desired.

symbols

cut ——————

front ——————
score

soft —·—·—·—
score

back ···········
score

G

Swan

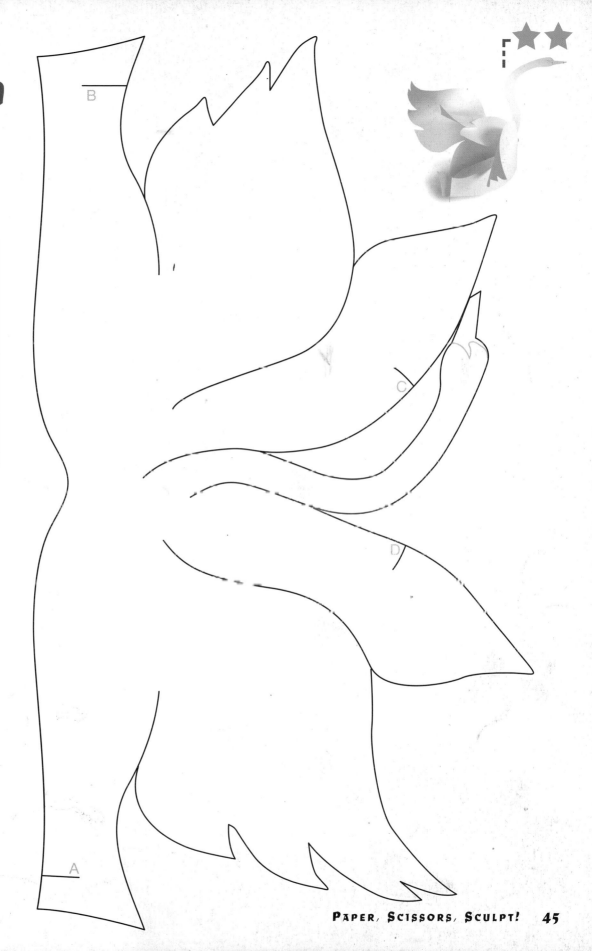

Swan ★★

1 Copy the pattern.

2 Cut the pattern out.

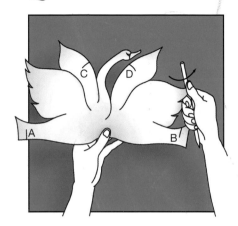

3 BACK VIEW: Bend both wings in a gentle curve.

4 BACK VIEW: Bend the body in an egg shape curve. Use a pencil or fingers in short strokes.

5 BACK VIEW: Insert slit A into slit B.

6 BACK VIEW: Insert slit C into slit D.

7 BACK VIEW: Push down linked CD between wings very gently.

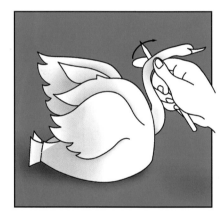

8 SIDE VIEW: Bend the neck so that it faces the front.

Nature and Paper Sculpture

Nature builds with complex functional forms. We can only simulate the wonders of nature.

Paper will not stand on the edge.

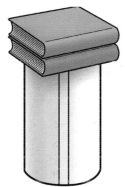

Rolled into a tube, it will stand up.

Tape up the edges. How many books will it support?

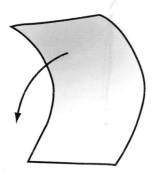

Compare it with tree trunks . . .

or hollow bamboo stalks . . .

and delicate mushroom stems.

Scoring paper makes it possible to create art.

Accordion-folded paper.

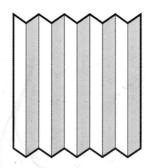

Compare it with a scallop shell.

Rabbit

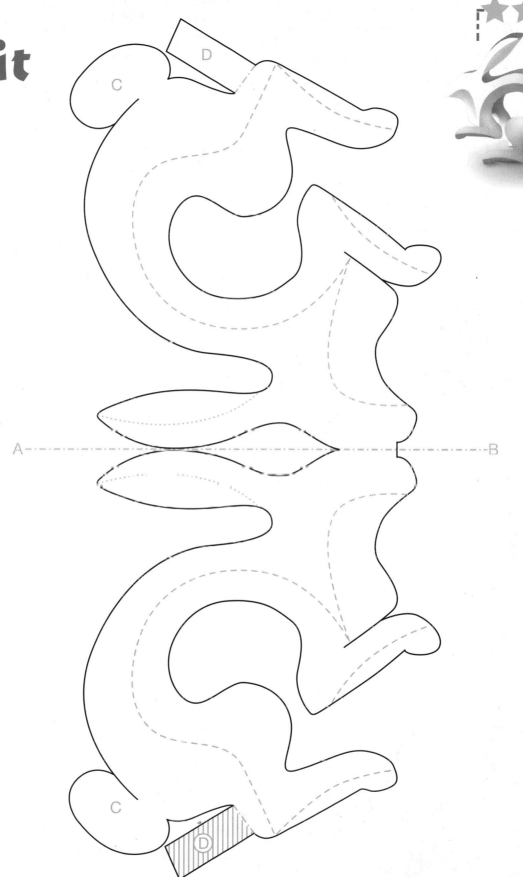

supplies

80 lb. paper
scissors
color

symbols

cut	——
front score	- - - -
back score	....
soft score	-·-·-·-
glue area	/////////

Rabbit ★★★

1 Copy the pattern at the same size. Transfer the back score.

2 Cut along the outline of the pattern.

3 Score the front and back.

4 Bend the front and back scores carefully.

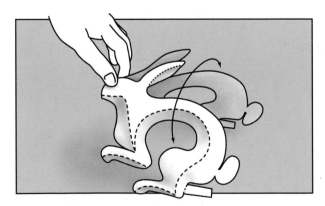

5 Fold the score AB sharply by pinching the head. This will bring the two halves together.

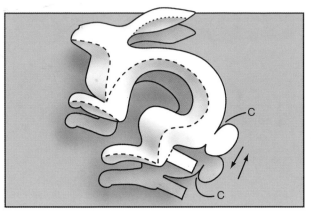

6 Insert the two tail slits C into each other.

7 Glue the tie-tabs D. Make them overlap fully.

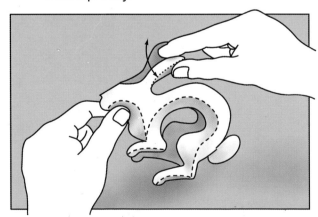

8 Finally, rebend the scores. Bend the ears out.

9 To color: Do not glue in step 7. Flatten the pattern and apply color. Then proceed with steps 7 and 8.

Squirrel

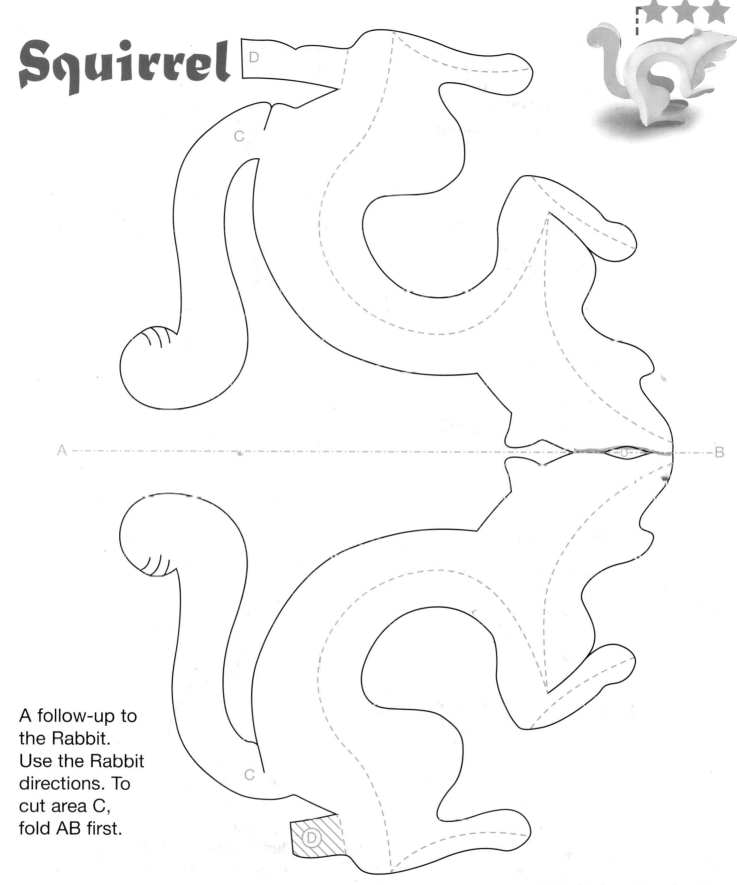

A follow-up to the Rabbit. Use the Rabbit directions. To cut area C, fold AB first.

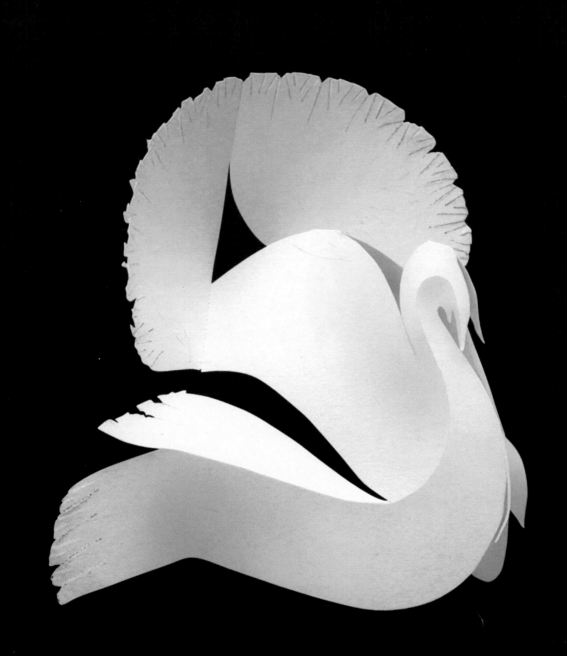

Turkey

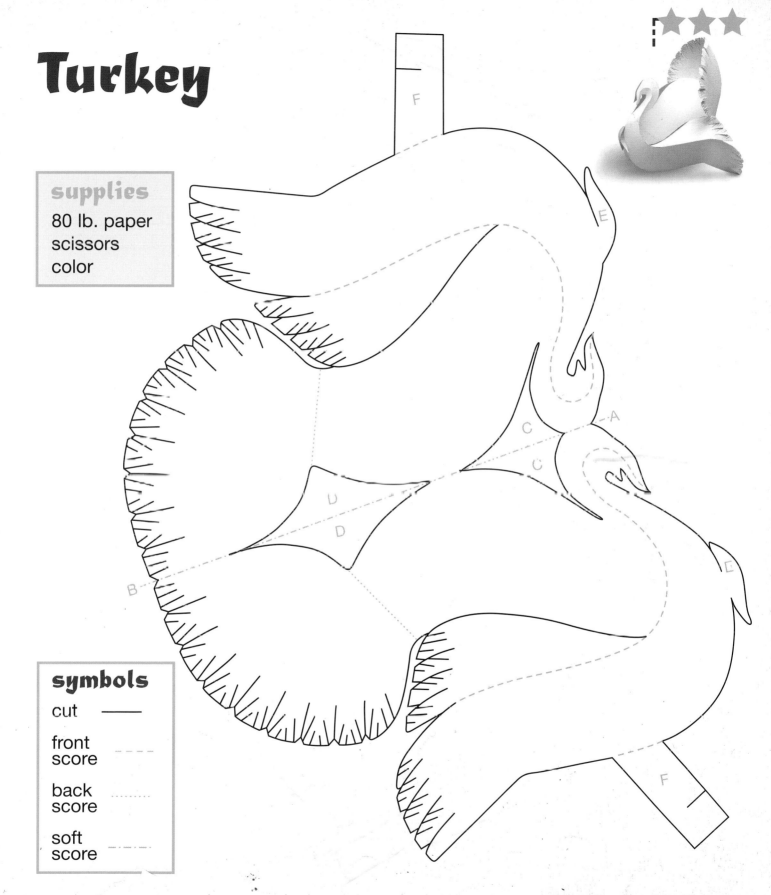

supplies

80 lb. paper
scissors
color

F

E

C · A

C

D

D

B

E

F

symbols

cut ———

front
score - - - - -

back
score · · · · · ·

soft
score - · - · -

Turkey ★★★

1 Copy the pattern

2 Transfer the back scores.

3 Soft score AB.

4 Fold AB and crease carefully.

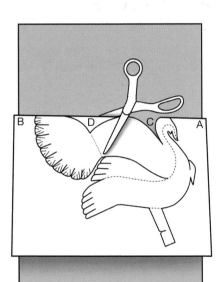

5 Keep the paper folded. Cut out parts C and D carefully.

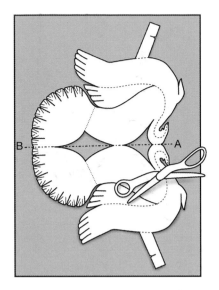

6 Open the pattern flat. Cut out the rest. Score it.

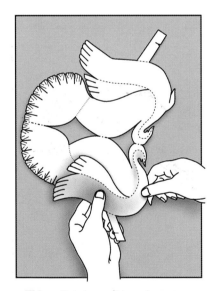

7 Bend the paper along all the score lines.

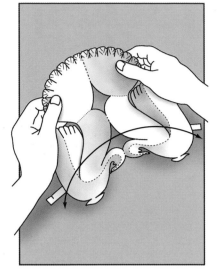

8 Holding both sides of the tail, bend it toward you, so it stands up. The body folds at the same time (see arrow).

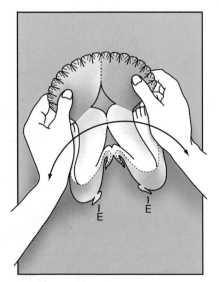

9 Continue this motion until the beards E come together and touch.

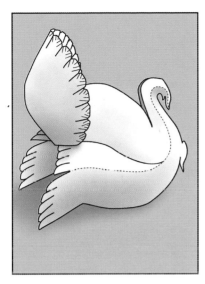

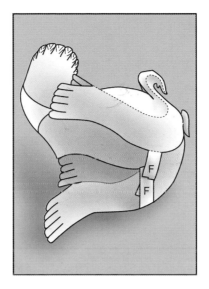

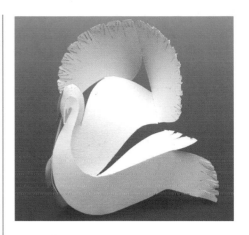

10 As the beards E come together, the tail should stand up like this.

12 BOTTOM VIEW: Hook up the tabs F carefully. The tab ends must be inside.

14 To color: Set the Turkey up to sense the color relationship in three dimensions. Then flatten it and color. Follow up with the Peacock.

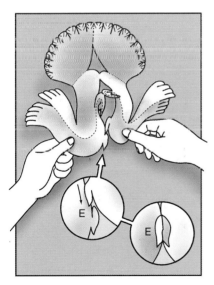

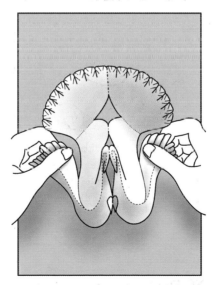

11 Carefully lift up one side of the body to line up the slits. Hook the beards E together.

13 Bend the wings in a gentle curve. Ruffle the feathers by separating the cuts.

Peacock

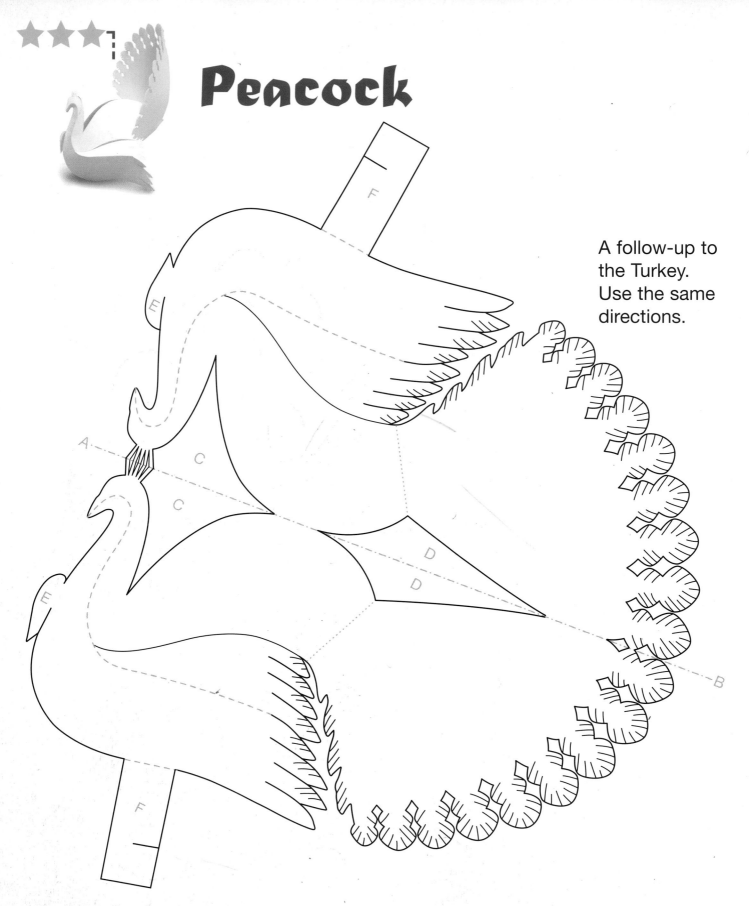

A follow-up to the Turkey. Use the same directions.

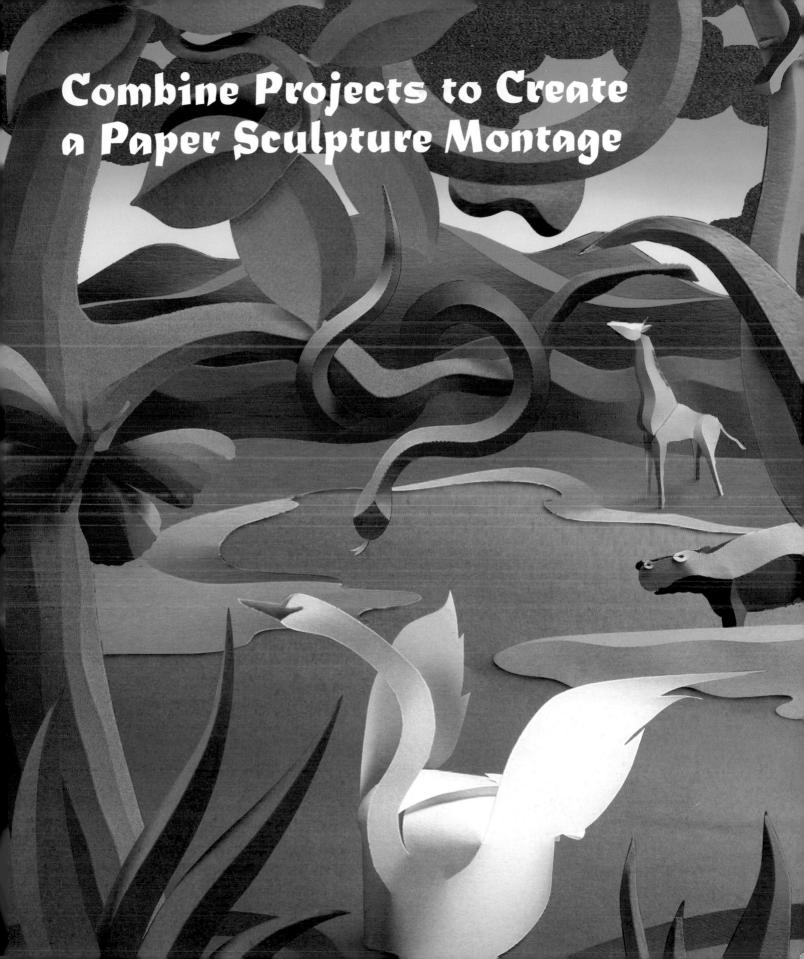

Combine Projects to Create
a Paper Sculpture Montage

Duck

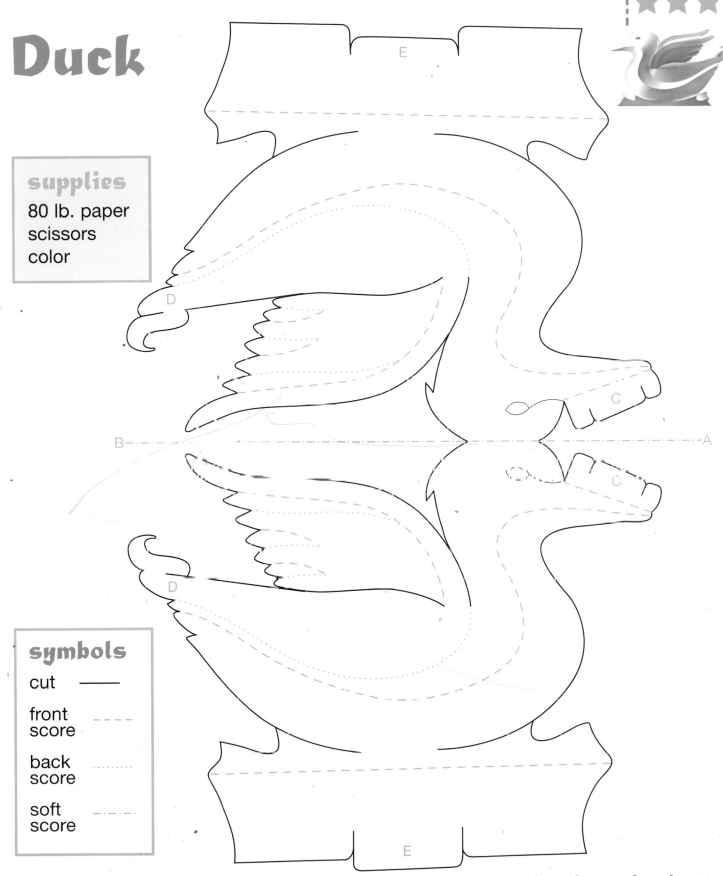

symbols

cut ——————

front
score ‑ ‑ ‑ ‑ ‑

back
score ·············

soft
score ‑·‑·‑·‑·

E

D

C

B ——————————————————————————— A

C

D

E

Duck ★ ★ ★

1 Copy the pattern at the same size.

2 Transfer the back scores.

3 Cut the pattern out.

4 Score the whole pattern.

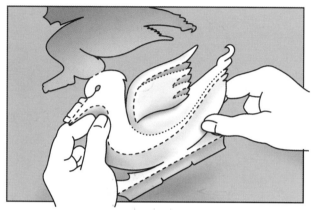

5 Bend the scores carefully. Note the scores on the wings.

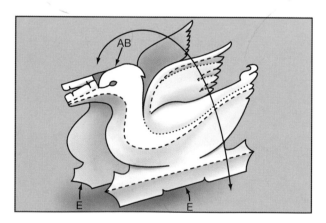

6 Bend score lines AB until tabs E overlap.

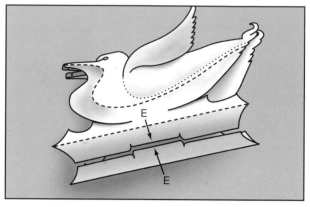

7 BOTTOM VIEW: Insert the two E tabs into each other.

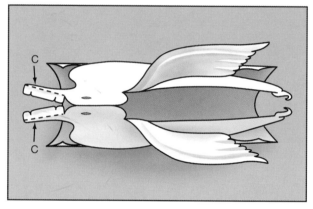

8 TOP VIEW: Insert the two C beak tabs into each other.

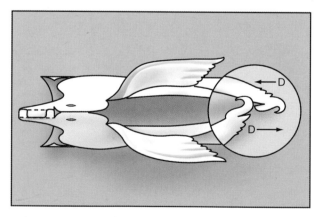

9 TOP VIEW: Insert the two D tail tabs into each other.

10 Ruffle the feathers. Flare out the wings. Flatten to color. Follow up with the Pelican on the next page.

Pelican

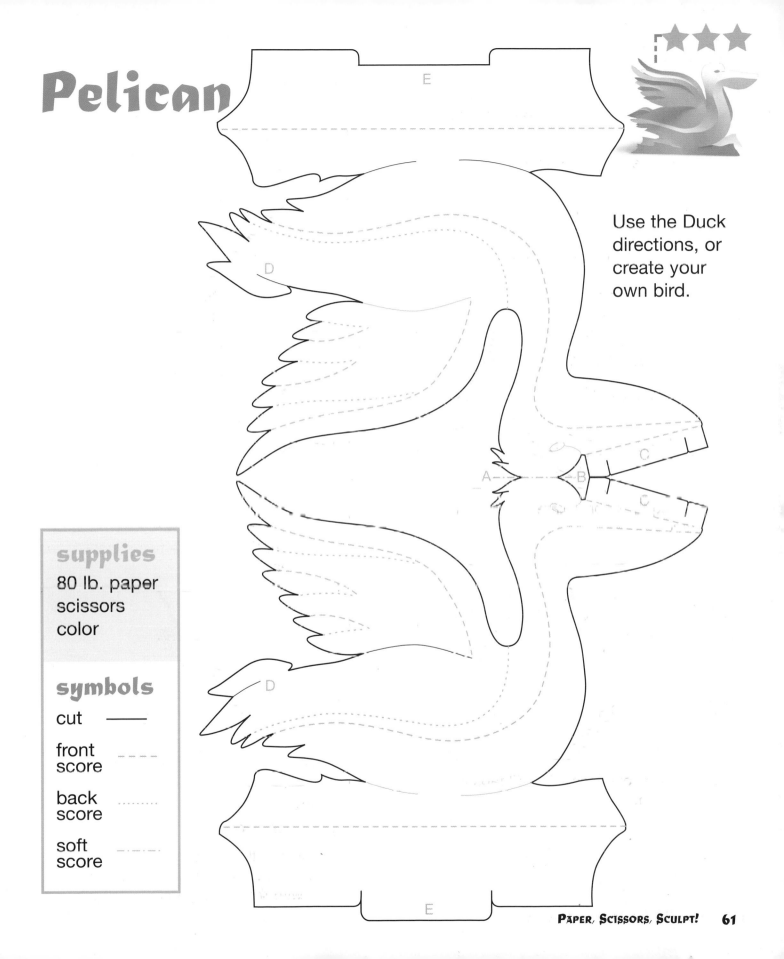

Use the Duck directions, or create your own bird.

Tyrannosaurus Rex

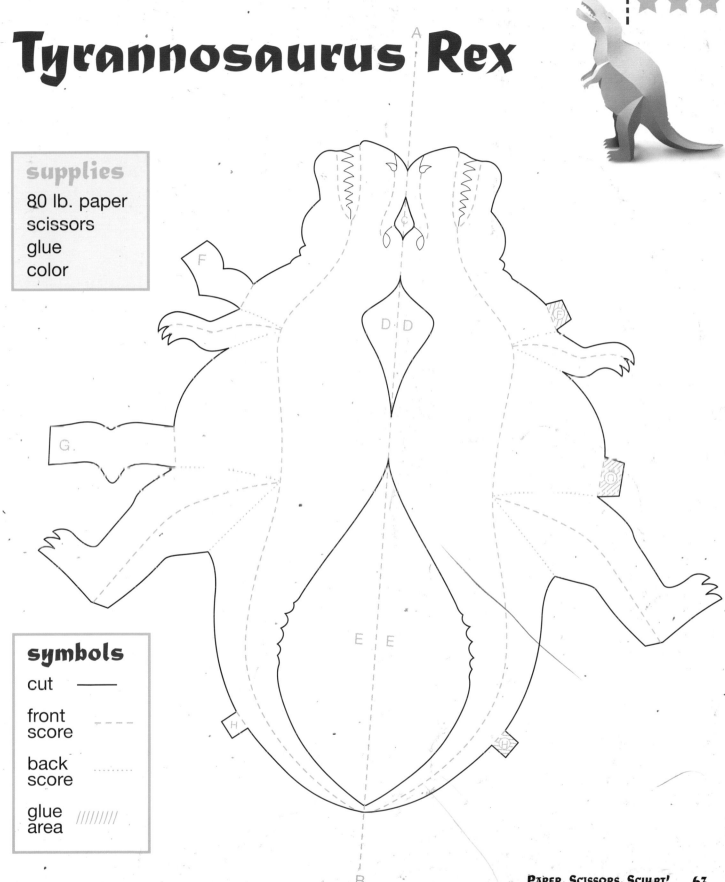

supplies

80 lb. paper
scissors
glue
color

symbols

cut ⎯⎯⎯⎯

front
score - - - - -

back
score ·········

glue
area //////////

Tyrannosaurus Rex ★★★

1 Copy the pattern. You may want to enlarge it by about 50 percent.

2 Transfer the back scores.

3 Score AB. Fold carefully.

4 Keep it folded. Cut out parts C, D, and E.

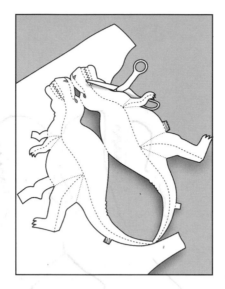

5 Open it flat. Cut the outline.

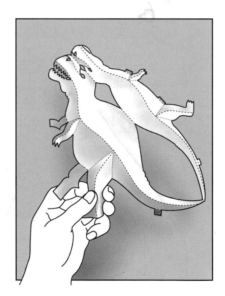

6 Score. Bend the scores carefully.

7 Fold body along AB.

8 Color as desired, before gluing in Step 9.

9 Glue tab G first, then H and F.

Creative Dinosaur

Design Your Own Creative Dinosaur Pattern

This is a combination follow-up to the T-Rex and the Stegosaurus (following page). Starting with the T-Rex pattern as a guide, try to create your own original dinosaur pattern. Use techniques that you learn from the Stegosaurus and previous lessons.

supplies
80 lb. paper
tracing paper
pencil
scissors
glue, color

Directions

1 Lightly trace one side of the T-Rex pattern.

2 Draw your own creative design over the T-Rex pattern.

3 Score and fold the center line of the white paper.

4 Keep it folded and cut both sides at the same time following your design on the tracing paper.

5 Remove tracing paper. Open the pattern. Score, bend and assemble it.

6 If it doesn't work out right the first time, don't be discouraged. Designing is a process of trial and error. Rework the pattern until you perfect your original design.

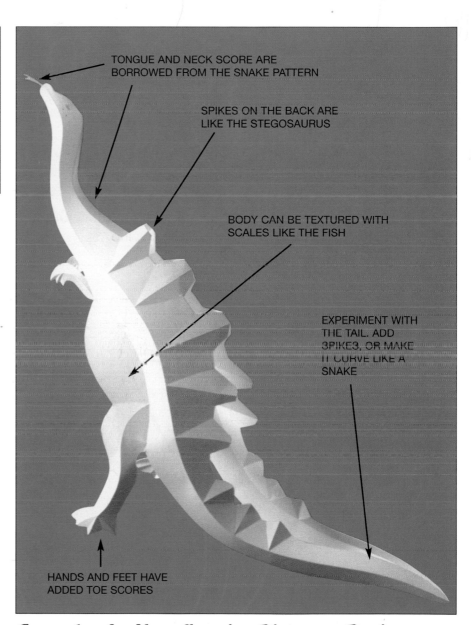

TONGUE AND NECK SCORE ARE BORROWED FROM THE SNAKE PATTERN

SPIKES ON THE BACK ARE LIKE THE STEGOSAURUS

BODY CAN BE TEXTURED WITH SCALES LIKE THE FISH

EXPERIMENT WITH THE TAIL. ADD SPIKES, OR MAKE IT CURVE LIKE A SNAKE

HANDS AND FEET HAVE ADDED TOE SCORES

Example of a New Creative Dinosaur Design

Stegosaurus

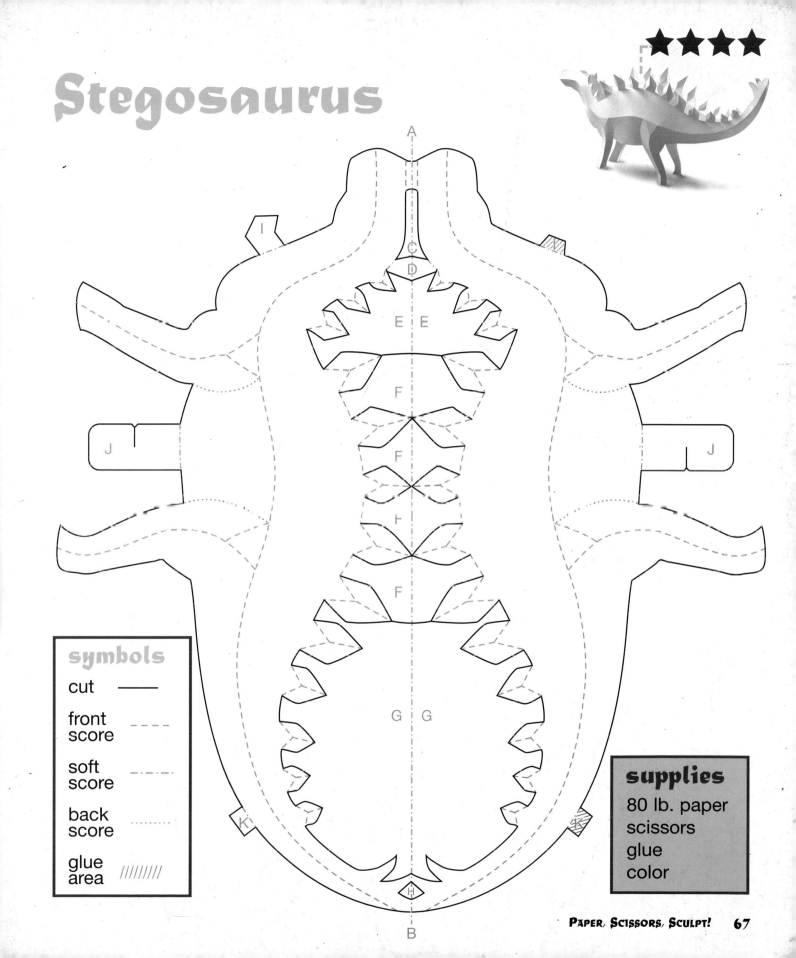

symbols

cut ———

front
score - - - -

soft
score - · - · -

back
score · · · · ·

glue
area //////////

supplies

80 lb. paper
scissors
glue
color

Stegosaurus ★★★★

1 Copy the pattern.

2 Soft score AB. You may want to use a ruler to guide the scissors.

3 Fold AB carefully. Crease.

4 Refold AB the opposite way. Crease.

5 Again refold AB the opposite way to expose the pattern. Crease.

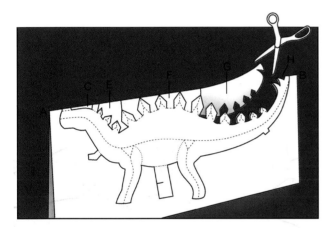

6 Keep the pattern folded. Cut out parts, C, E, G, and H.

7 *Cut into* the ribs (F) carefully.

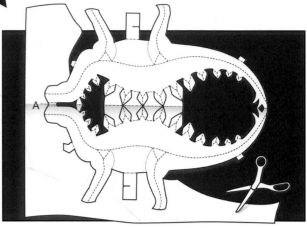

8 Open the pattern flat. Cut out the rest of the pattern.

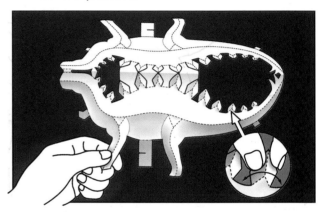

9 Fold the straight scores. Bend the curve scores. Pinch-bend the plate scores *(see enlarged detail)*.

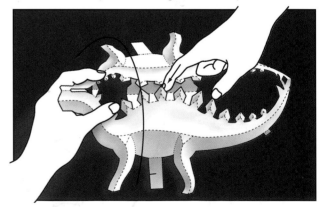

10 To fold the body and the ribs at the same time, fold the body with one hand and, at the same time, push down the ribs with the forefinger of the other hand. Do this simultaneously. Move slowly and gently.

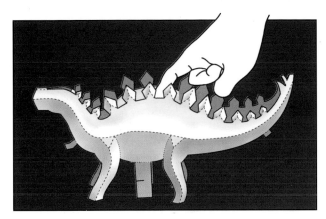

11 Continue this motion along the ribs.

12 Finally, press the two sides together so that the rib scores are fully folded inside the body.

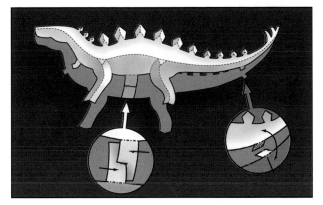

13 Optional: Flatten the model and color.

14 Rebend all the scores gently.

15 Glue tail tabs K and chest tabs I.

16 Fasten the belly tabs J. Tab ends must be on the inside.

17 Bend out the plates a bit. Stand the finished sculpture up.

Kangaroo

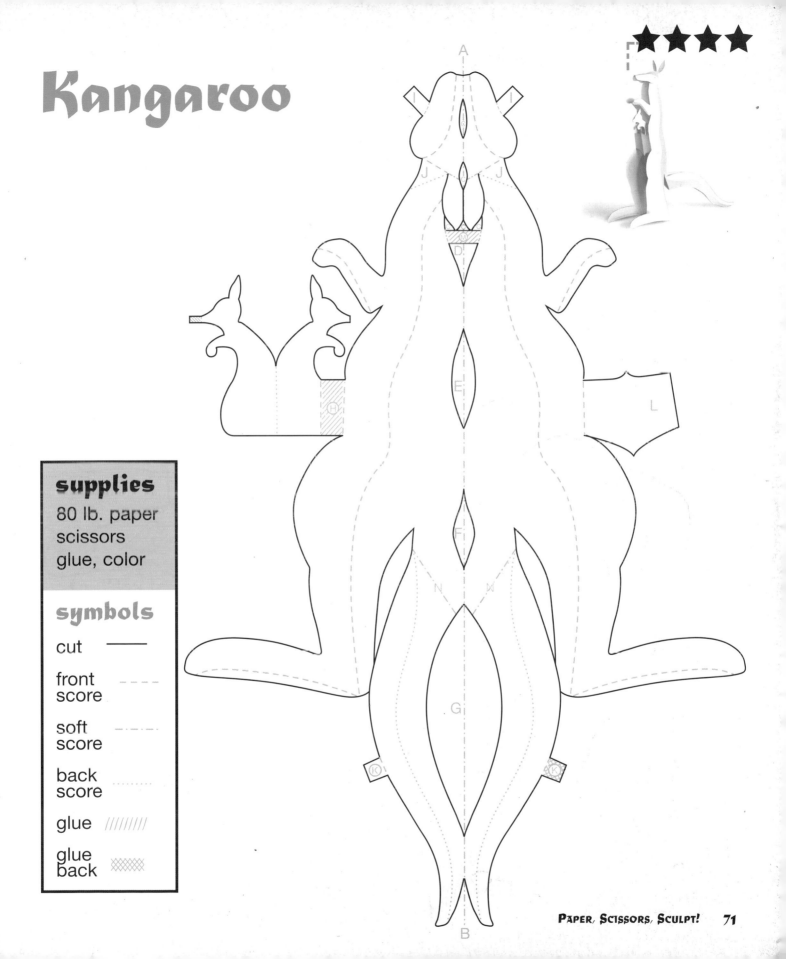

★★★★

supplies

80 lb. paper
scissors
glue, color

symbols

cut ——————

front
score   — — — —

soft
score   — · — · —

back
score   · · · · · · ·

glue   /////////

glue
back   ✕✕✕✕✕

A

I   I

J   J   J

D

E

F

N   N

G

H

L

K   K

B

Kangaroo ★★★★

1. Copy the pattern at the same size or enlarge, up to 150 or 200 percent with thicker paper.

2. Transfer the back scores.

3. Soft score AB.

4. Fold AB and crease it carefully.

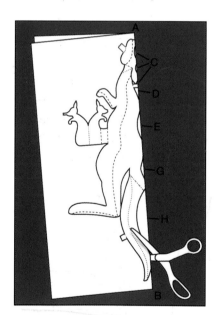

5. Keep the paper folded. Cut out C, D, E, F, and G.

6. Open the pattern and cut it out. Score it.

7. BACK VIEW: Optional to color. Paint both sides.

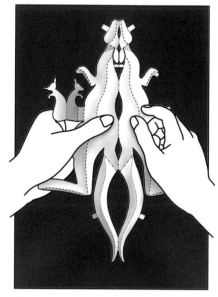

8. Bend all the scores very carefully.

9. Fold the body and, at the same time, fold the tail.

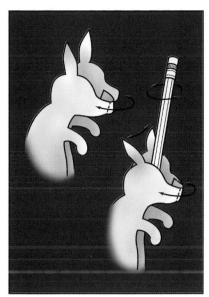

10 Glue the baby 'Roo's nose tab. Twirl a pencil inside the baby 'Roo to shape it. Bend out the ears.

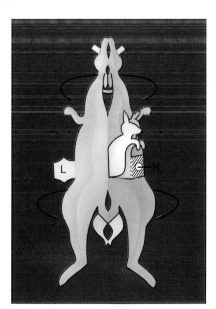

11 FRONT VIEW: Glue the apron L to H very carefully.

12 To fold in the neck joint J, push the head down gently, so that the neck joint slides under the jaw. Glue the I tabs together.

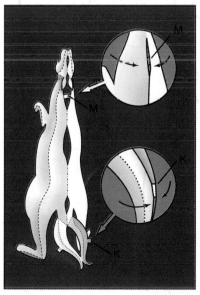

13 BACK VIEW: Glue the shoulder tab M and the tail tabs K.

14 Fold up the ears. Rebend all the scores gently. Spread the legs and set the figure up. It may lean forward or backward. To change posture, refold score N.

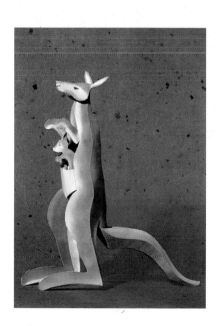

Snail

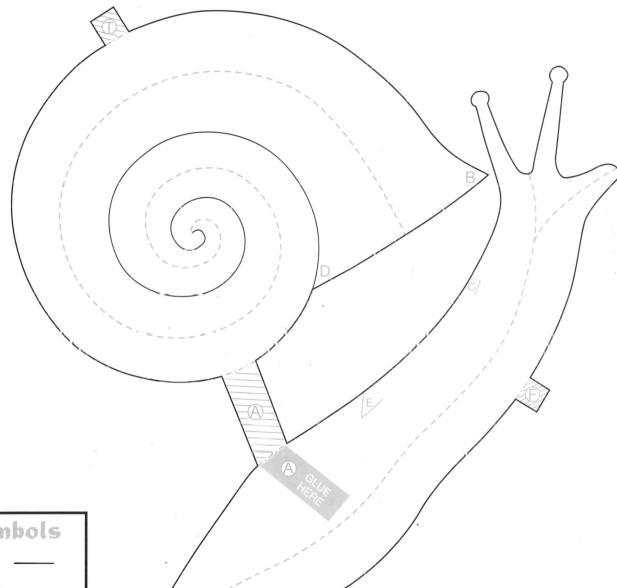

symbols

cut	——————
front score	– – – – –
soft score	··············
glue area	//////////

supplies

80 lb. paper
scissors
glue
color

 **Snail** ★★★★

1 Copy the pattern at the same size or larger.

2 Score the whole pattern.

3 OPTION: Color as desired now.

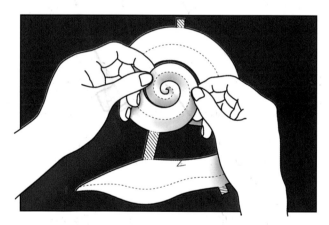

4 To bend the shell scores, start from the center whorl and gently bend scores in a circular motion.

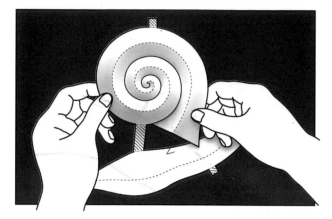

5 Repeat the circular bending motion until there is enough depth to the whorl.

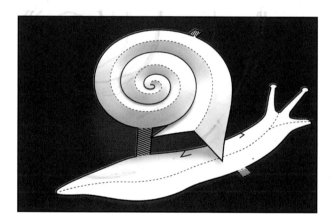

6 Maximize the curves to allow it to spring back. Repeat gently.

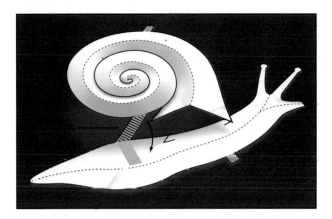

7 Attach the shell to the body by bending A forward. Glue to the spot indicated on the pattern.

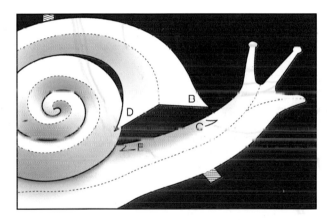

8 Put glue on the underside of point D. Stick it to E. Let dry. Do the same to glue B to C. Let dry.

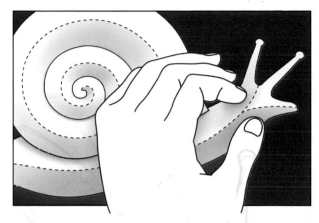

9 Bend the scores on the snail body. Gently pinch the head a bit to give it more dimension.

10 To mount the snail for display:
1. Fold tab T and tab F under the snail.
2. Mark tab T position on the mounting surface with a pencil.
3. Unfold tab T and apply glue. Fold tab T and press to glue. Let dry thoroughly.
4. Bend snail scores to give it dimension. Mark new position of tab F on the mounting surface.
5. Unfold tab F. Apply glue. Fold under and press down to stick at the pencil mark position.

Giraffe

supplies

80 lb. paper
scissors
glue, color

symbols

cut ——————

front
score — — — —

back
score ·············

glue ///////

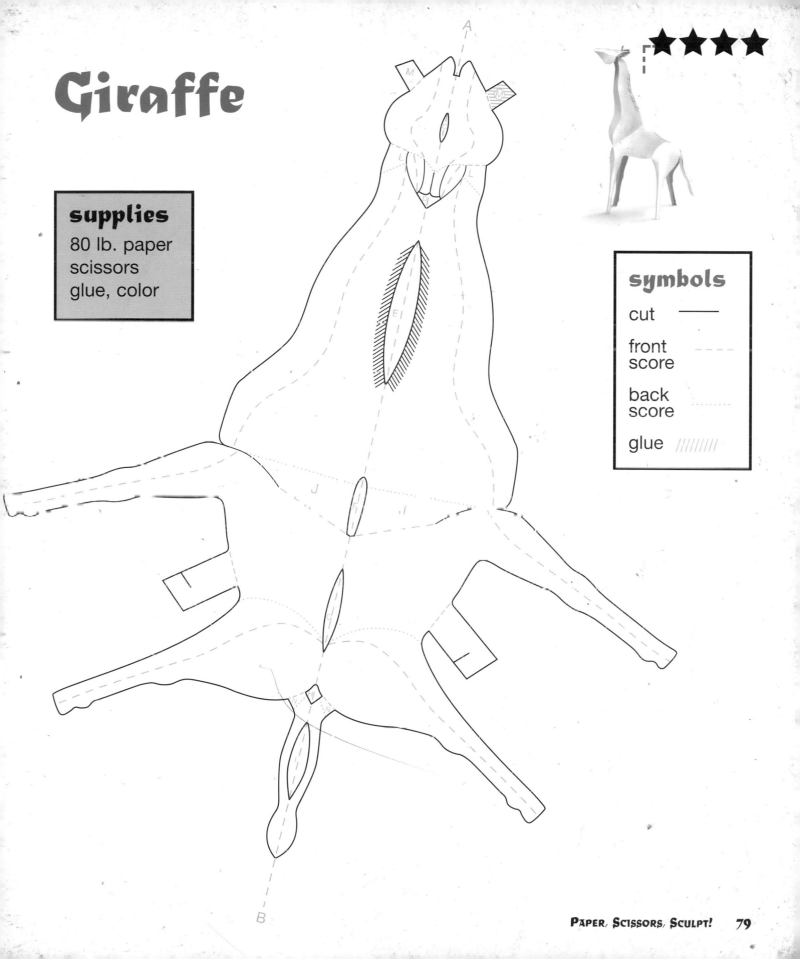

Giraffe ★★★★

1 Copy the pattern at the same size or enlarge it.

2 Transfer the back scores.

3 Score AB and fold the pattern. Crease.

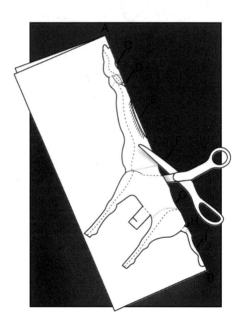

4 Keep the pattern folded. Cut out C, D, E, F, G, H, and I.

5 Cut into the mane with short diagonal cuts.

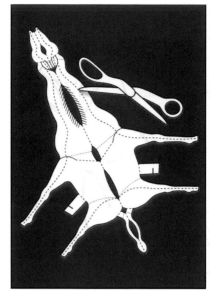

6 Open the pattern and cut it out. Score it.

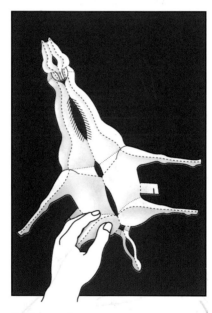

7 Bend all the scores carefully.

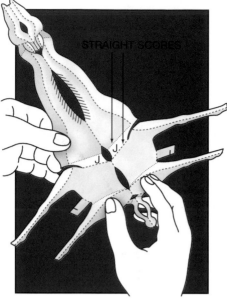

STRAIGHT SCORES

8 Pay special attention to the straight scores. Fold and crease them.

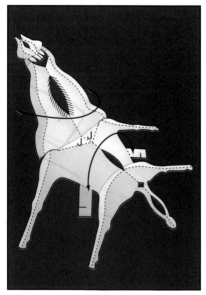

9 To make the neck bend upward, gently squeeze the neck and body while moving the neck upward. The J areas should bend inward.

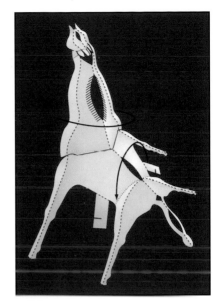

10 Continue this motion slowly and carefully until the J areas slip inside, and are completely hidden.

11 Continue until the legs are standing up.

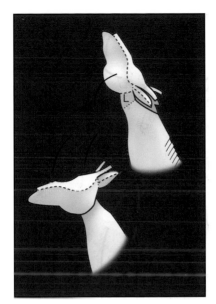

12 Fold the neck joint L by pushing the head down gently.

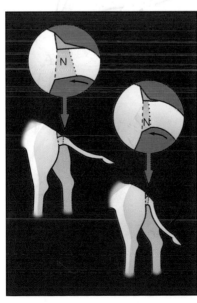

13 Fold in the tail joint N. The tail will move down. Pinch it flat.

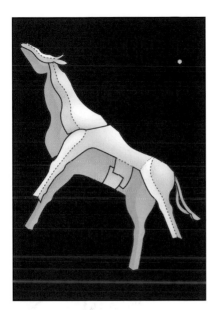

14 Optional: Color as desired. Flatten it, color and let it dry.

15 Rebend the scores gently. Bend up the horns and ears. Insert the belly tabs. Stand the sculpture up.

Gallery
One-piece Sculptures

Woolly Mammoth

This piece was a great opportunity to experiment with texture. I used a sharp mat knife to cut the fur. A tracing wheel added more texture. I had to be very careful when making the numerous cuts in the legs because too many would limit its structural integrity. The base was created with torn pieces of paper glued together. The mammoth is one piece of paper.

Pony

This is an early work. It is an interesting piece because it can fold flat. The saddle pushes down and it pops into shape. People find it hard to believe that it is one piece of paper until I show them the pattern. The next one will have a rider as well.

Mountain Goat

I've always been inspired by this animal's strength and agility. It seems dignified with its pristine white fur and beard. Because of the large amount of fur texture, the paper became more pliable. I was able to shape the body without actually scoring it. This gives the body a roundness.

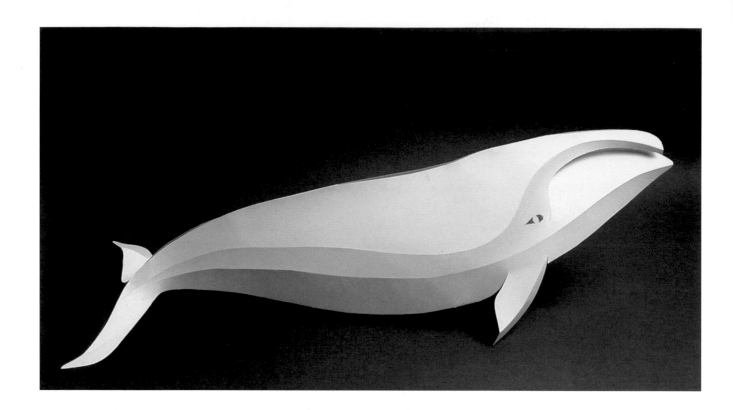

Blue Whale

This is a good example of form following function. Its long, streamlined body plumbs the mysterious ocean depths.

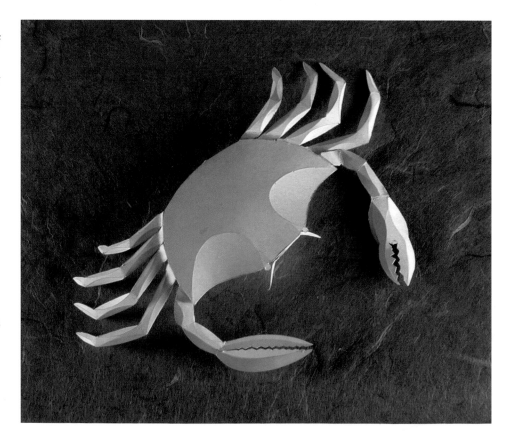

Crab

Like lobster and shrimp, the crab has an exoskeleton that makes it an ideal subject for paper sculpture. Its arms and body are broken down into geometric shapes. The curved scores help to round its back and hold the form.

Eagle with Fish

After seeing a program on eagles that feed on fish in Alaska, I was inspired to create a piece that would illustrate this dramatic encounter. The wings have small supports that keep them spread, and the base is weighted to keep it balanced.

Bat

This a more complex version than the one-star pattern presented in the beginning of the book. By using the skills acquired by following the directions, you can experiment and create your own custom versions of the projects.

Cricket

Of the many species of cricket, I chose this one for artistic reasons. Because of the fine hair-like antennae, I had to use a very sharp mat knife. The challenge was designing the three pairs of legs, and still keeping it as one piece of paper.

Dragon

I made many versions of this piece in the process of its development. I wanted it to be unique and original. I accomplished this by taking elements from the Chinese dragon and the medieval European dragon to create my own version. The tracing wheel was used for added texture.

Big Horn

Creating the horns in the one-piece format was the biggest challenge. Because of the small size (five inches high), I did not add more detail in the horns, although a larger pattern could incorporate many of the Gupit-Gupit[SM] techniques that are explained in this book.

Conic Variation

In experimenting with the cone shape, I happened upon this new and interesting variation that uses twisting angles and still retains the cone feeling.

Eagle

This is one of my earliest experimental works. It uses shaping techniques and cutouts to create the head and feathers.

Lantern

The Lantern began by experimentation. It has no scores and is made from thin but sturdy paper. I folded a strip of paper at different angles until I created this shape. I then taught it to my students, and they came up with their own original ideas. Once the lantern is made, it can be expanded or contracted in different ways to radically change the shape.

Horned Owl

I designed this piece with simplicity in mind. The head was cut using serrated scissors. I may use it or a variation of it in a future publication. It stands by balancing on the tail and wing tips.

Turtle

Over the years, I have worked on many different turtle ideas. I was never happy with them until I developed this one. The puzzling part was getting the thirteen back plates to come together and still be one piece. When this pattern finally evolved, I was surprised at its simplicity. I plan to create a giant Galapagos turtle, and possibly an alligator snapping turtle as well, with geometric pyramid shapes that protrude from its shell.

Frog

Paper does not stretch to form compound curves like those found in a ball. I used a combination of score lines to give the illusion of the curves in the frog's body.

Heron

I have always admired the beauty and grace of these birds. I bent the neck and the head with the fish downward, not only for artistic reasons, but also to help the two legs support the body. A later version, not shown, has a rocking base that enables the sculpture to tip forward and backward.

Triceratops

Designing the umbrella shape around the top of the head was the biggest challenge for this sculpture. This particular animal had many variations before it became extinct.

Sculptures from More than One Piece of Paper

The Maharaja

This is a very early piece that utilizes more than one piece of paper. I was experimenting with different ways of making a turban and tunic. My mother was a dressmaker and I learned a lot about clothing patterns from her. The figure is riding on an elephant (not shown).

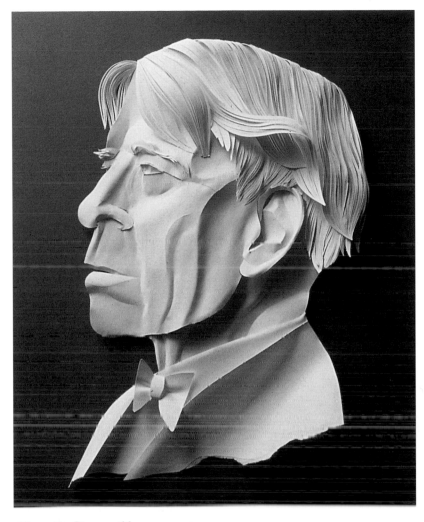

Carl Sandburg

This life size sculpture is a one-inch-deep relief, and was made using the techniques taught in this book. It was created from several pieces of paper. I did a series of portraits, experimenting with different angles (profile, three quarter view, and front). I began experimenting with thin-gauge copper, and went on to create a portrait of Marian Anderson.

Cowboy

This work was made from three pieces of paper. I was able to bring out the nose by folding the paper into the narrow channel on the upper lip. The fully three-dimensional face extends upward and becomes the top of the hat. The brim was dropped over it. The scarf was added to the bottom.

Glossary

Back score Paper is scored on the back side.

Crease To go over a straight score with the thumb or a ruler so as to get a sharp edge.

Front score Paper is scored on the front side of the paper.

Score To mark or scribe the paper with a sharp point of the scissors or a mat knife to enable bending of a straight or curved line.

Soft score The paper is scored by a dull tool like the point of a closed scissors, table knife, hard pencil, etc. The paper fibers are compressed, not cut. The soft score is stronger and can be bent or folded both ways without breaking.

Texture The smooth, plain paper surface has been altered by a tool such as a tracing wheel that can produce a tactile effect.

Tie-tab A projection that binds or connects one part of a paper sculpture to another part.

The Paper Clinic

Q. Why doesn't the paper bend easily on the score line?

A. The score is probably not deep enough. Try adding a little more pressure with the tool when scoring.

Q. Why does the score line seem weak and bend too easily?

A. The score line is too deep. Apply less pressure with the tool.

Q. What should I do if I accidentally cut through the paper?

A. Use a small piece of transparent tape on the back side to repair it.

Q. How do I get my curve scores to bend neatly?

A. Assuming that the score depth is okay, the score must be bent gently, going one small section at a time. Do not attempt to bend it completely the first time. Bend the score line from beginning to end and then repeat until the desired effect is obtained. Patience and practice are the keys to success.

Q. How can I work with decorative papers that are too thin?

A. Thinner papers can be laminated to thicker papers using spray glue. Apply the glue to the thicker paper.

Index

About the Author

Ben A. Gonzales has had a lifelong interest in early childhood art education. His research papers include "The Gifted Child," and "Student Opinion Of Teacher Performance." He is a licensed examiner in art for the Board of Education in New York City and he designed the rating chart for sculpture. His work in paper and other media has been displayed and used in workshops, advertising, and illustrations. He had national

exposure on Fred Rogers' children's television program, *Mr. Rogers' Neighborhood*. After high school in the Philippines, he majored in graphic arts at Cooper Union Art School and received an MS in art education from Hunter College. He taught for many years at the High School of Art and Design in New York City.